MARKETPLACE LEADERSHIP CAPSULES

30 Fundamental Reflections for Leadership Success and Management Development.

DR CHARLES OMOLE

Copyright 2017
Charles Omole

Published by: Winning Faith

WINNING FAITH
OUTREACH MINISTRIES

London . New York . Lagos

ISBN: 978-1-907095-24-5

DEDICATION

This book is dedicated to all current and aspiring leaders labouring daily in the world; Do not give up, as your labour will be rewarded.

INTRODUCTION

A Capsule is a form of dispensing medications. This book is about some fundamental prescriptions that will help you become the best leader you can be in the Marketplace. They are reflections that are intended to shape your thinking and challenge your paradigms, while building your leadership capabilities.

As a Christian, I will be taking many inspirations from the Bible for some of the reflections discussed in this book. This is not a religious book in any form; I am merely revealing my personal source of leadership inspiration to affirm my overarching influence in relation to what great leadership should look like.

So if you are not a Christian, you will still be informed and challenged by this book. Despite the many references to Bible characters in this introduction; most of the book is focused on sound universal management principles all can relate with.

The leadership principles and reflections in this book, will work in any area of life where you are a leader. From project managers, entrepreneurs, CEOs and team managers to leaders of Charitable and Religious institutions.

The reflections will help you in every corporate environment and any sector in the Marketplace you function in. Also my use of the male pronoun "he" in some areas of the book is not intended to depict male only. It is for ease of reading but females are also included.

There are many books on the subject of leadership already in existence. So I decided this will not just be another book with long sentences. Rather I will like this to be a book of reflections. Hence a quote followed by my analysis and then yours own opportunity to pen your views.

This book is a call for you to pause and reflect on what leadership mean to you and how you are fulfilling your role and mandate as a leader. How effective are you? The field of leadership scholarship is full of thousands of books that breaks down the subject into technical details and its many dimensions.

Hence my aim in this book is to help the leadership practitioner to reflect on key philosophical meditations on leadership, its operation, contradictions, burden and rewards. Over the last few decades; there appears to be a leadership paradigm that has developed in many cultures which is purely transactional in nature.

That is, leadership that merely use people, rather than develop them. Of course many followers also use leaders. This reality has led to unhealthy developments in the global socio-political leadership landscape, with worship and adoration of men/women in leadership rampant and common place.

As the demand for this transactional outlook of leadership increases all over the world; many leaders have played along and fed this outrage with ever increasing self-empire building and cult of personality that has consequently led to the breakdown of many followers when the leaders fall or are found wanting in some areas.

The truth is leaders are not perfect people. In fact, a study of the Christian Bible reveal many leaders God used mightily (Kings, Prophets, Priests & Apostles) in scriptures had one flaw and weakness or another.

In the Bible, starting with Abraham who lied to the King of Egypt, Isaac did the same; Jacob we know for his deception, Moses was a murderer, Aaron was a double agent, serving God and then building golden image for the people to worship. David was an adulterer and killer. And the Apostles were not spared either.

The New Testament[1] reveals Apostle Paul's own acceptance of weakness and the need for grace. Paul's obsession in this letter[2] is with how unimpressive he is, or at least with the fact that the only impressive thing about him is his weakness.

---

[1] In the Bible
[2] The book of 2 Corinthians

In this rambling apologia for his life and work as an apostle, Paul's weakness is the recurring theme. In chapter 4, for example, Paul writes of the glory of God revealed in the gospel and of his own call to be a minister of that gospel, when the glory of God in Christ shone in his heart.[3]

But the thought of the glory and the power of the gospel entrusted to him immediately, by contrast, suggests the thought of his own frailty: *'We have this treasure in earthen vessels'* (4: 7). The clay pot is both a very ordinary and a very fragile container for treasure.

What makes this theme of the apostle's weakness so arresting and intriguing is that Paul is not in the least apologising for it or mentioning it only for the sake of honesty. In chapters 11-12 of the same book (with deliberate irony, of course) Paul boasts of it, as precisely the qualification which validates his claim to be an Apostle of Christ.

He catalogues his sufferings,[4] not as heroic ordeals, but as evidence of how his ministry was marked by the physical and psychological frailty

---

[3] 2 Corinthians 4:3-7
[4] 2 Corinthians 11:23-33

of an ordinary human being, ending the catalogue with a vivid memory of the humiliating occasion when he had to flee for his life from Damascus by being lowered in a basket from the city wall.[5]

This weakness of Paul was the occasion for the power of God to be active and evident in his ministry: *'We have this treasure in earthen vessels, to show that the transcendent power belongs to God and not to us'* (4: 7); *'I will all the more gladly boast of my weaknesses, that the power of Christ may rest upon me'* (12: 9).

The power of God evident in Paul's ministry, not least in the transforming effect of the Gospel he preached, could be seen to be no mere human achievement of Paul's but divine power which found its opportunity in Paul's weakness. In his weakness Paul was obliged to trust in God and his converts to recognise God.

One example Paul gives is the arrival of Titus, after a worrying delay, with unexpectedly good news about affairs in the church at Corinth (7: 5-7; note the echoes of the language of 1: 3-7). In

[5] ibid

2Cor. 4: 8-9 Paul gives a rhetorical list of 'cross' and 'resurrection' aspects of his experience:
"We are afflicted in every way, but not crushed; perplexed, but not driven to despair; persecuted, but not forsaken; struck down, but not destroyed".

The demands of his ministry had almost proved too much for him, but, by God's grace, not quite. Thus Paul's experience might often seem outwardly unremarkable. But because he sees the death and resurrection of Jesus as the key to his life, as to everything else, he can find there a pattern which makes Christian sense of his experience.

The shape which everyone needs to give to his experience in order to understand it Paul found in the cross and resurrection of Jesus. This pattern, however, was more than an interpretation of the experience: it also made the experience what it was for Paul.

To identify with Paul's experience, we do not need to be shipwrecked or imprisoned or lowered in a basket from a city wall. Even without the physical dangers of Paul's career, anyone who throws himself into the work of Christian ministry of any kind with half the dedication of Paul will experience the weakness of which Paul speaks.

The times when problems seem insoluble, the times of weariness from sheer overwork, the times of depression when there seem to be no results, the emotional exhaustion which pastoral concern can bring on - in short, all the times when the leader knows he has stretched to the limits of his capacities for a task which is very nearly, but by God's grace not quite, too much for him.

Anyone who knows only his strength, not his weakness, has never given himself to a task which demands all he can give. There is no avoiding this weakness, and we should learn to suspect those traditional and institutional models of human life which try to avoid it.

We should no longer be taken-in by the ideal of the charismatic superman Leader, with a constant source of superhuman strength. We have seen too many examples of leaders who seem to promote loyalty to themselves through a pretentious appearance of perfection and infallibility.

This has led to some leaders becoming God in people's lives. This unhealthy relationship therefore kills the leadership drive in many people as they seek to escape from this unattainable utopia of leadership perfection. This is wrong.

Life is breaking this cult of personality worship by allowing the uncovering of the weaknesses of some leaders so that people can see that God alone should be their worship; even though we love, respect and support our leaders. We must know that the best of leader are still humans with weaknesses.

Nobody wants to work with a perfect leader. You need to build collaboration and solidarity by revealing your weaknesses as validation of the humanity of yourself as a Leader.

To be controlled by the love of Christ means inevitably to reach the limits of one's abilities and experience weakness. Of course, I am not suggesting that the Leader should not take sensible precautions against overwork or reasonable steps to maintain his physical and mental health.

Nor am I suggesting he should not do his best to be efficient in his work. He owes it to himself to do so. But a transformational perspective on service takes us further than that.

The leader should be sensible, but above all he must be wholehearted. He should try to be efficient, but even when his efficiency runs out, the effectiveness of his actions need not do so. His efficiency may actually need sometimes to run out (by necessity), not neglect - if the power of God is to prove effective in his activities.

That the leader's life should match his message is a common enough thought. For many, the leader's weakness is not the point where he is failing per se, but the point where the deepest integration of his personal life and his teaching/message is possible.

So what is the summary of what I have been saying and what this book is trying to convey:
- That Leaders are not Perfect; so you can be a leader you are destined to be.

- That the more perfect a Leader tries to pretend to be; the more strongly we should be careful. A leader who has seen the grace and mercy of God manifest in his weaknesses; will show humility, empathy and love while still upholding the unchanging Truth as standard. You condemn more if you have not worked in other's shoes; and perhaps you may be guilty of the same offence.

- Followers who live with the perception of a *"perfect and flawless"* leader; will be grossly disappointed in the current dispensation. When such leaders fall; the followers are disproportionately badly affected. Our focus should not be on the personalities. Circumstances are getting rid of super star leaders and promoting stable servant leaders.

- You must not be discouraged from going into leadership or performing your leadership duties simply because you are work-in-progress in certain areas of life. Your weaknesses, once given to God; should not stop you from performing as a

Leader. God will still back you up with all his resources.

- If we see God as the only perfect personality and leaders as merely vessels called to do a certain task or lead a defined mission; we will be better able to accept their fallibilities and weaknesses.

This book has been produced as quotes for reflection, rather than long written texts of a normal book. This is partly why this introduction has been long; to set up the stage for the rest of the book. The vision is to produce a set of leadership quotes that you can read and reflect upon from time to time.

The purpose is to fortify you and encourage you to make good on your leadership journey. You can be the best leader in the world; despite your weaknesses. So as a good leader, focus on the assignment you have been given or gaols you seek to achieve. When you do this you will succeed, regardless of the weakness you are working through.

That is why God can give to Moses[6] (a Murderer), a tablet of Laws that include ... *"You shall not Kill"*. There is no contradiction here. The truth does not weaken or become obsolete, simply because a flawed vessel is publishing it.

This book contains some of the key statements I have used to train leaders for many years. The quotes are titled Leadership Capsules. They are then followed by my reflection on how each quote affects leadership development and capabilities. My reflections are my considered analysis of how each quote can shape your leadership development.

At the end of each Capsule; there is then an opportunity for you to write down your own reflections for your future reference and learning. In that sense, this is not a book you can lend someone else after reading. If done properly, it should contain so many personal reflections from you that it will become a leadership development "Bible" for you.

---

[6] A Bible character that led the children of Israel out of the captivity of Egypt.

At the end of the book, I am hoping you will score yourself out of thirty to see how many of the capsules you are proficient in and how many you still need work in. This should form part of a personal leadership development plan for you.

Reflect deeply on your journey so far in the court of leadership as you read these pages. I believe you can be the best leader in any area of life you find yourself. So congratulations and welcome to the first day of the rest of your life. I will see you at the top.

With much love always.

Dr Charles Omole,
2017

PROLOGUE

The Leadership Secret of a Lion.

The Lion is not the Tallest, Brightest, Quickest, Most Powerful, Biggest animal in the Jungle; yet it is the KING of the Jungle. The Lion is the King of the Jungle because of one important thing: **Attitude.**

The Lion has a different Attitude that makes all other animals Respect him. Hence, the number one element in effective Leadership is ATTITUDE.

What makes all these other bigger, stronger and taller animals Respect & Fear the Lion.... the ATTITUDE is the difference. For example; when the Lion sees an elephant...the first thing that comes to his mind is...LUNCH. So the Lion ACTS the way it THINKS.

That is, despite the elephant being bigger, stronger and taller than the Lion. This BOLDNESS conditions the Lion's attitude. The Lion then attacks the Elephant. Now the key is this: When the Elephant sees the Lion; the first thing that comes to his mind is...EATER IS HERE.

Consequently, the Elephant is CONTROLLED by the way he THINKS. He thinks that he is Lunch for the Lion. Therefore, his weight superiority, his Power, his bigger size, his Might have all become victims of the way he THINKS. When you have been defeated in your mind; nothing else matters. All advantages you possess become captives to your defeated mind-set.

So it does not matter how educated you are, how qualified you are; it's your mind that keeps you small. Just as it does not matter how small you, how unqualified and disadvantaged you are; it's your Mind that makes you a Leader.

The key is attitude. It is attitude that differentiates Leaders from Followers. Your attitude conditions your response and posture. Your attitude is a product of what you SEE.

Having the right attitude in life is important, but more so having the right attitude in leadership. Attitude is in the realm of choice, meaning that you can control it at any point in time, no matter the circumstances you are facing.

In fact, learning to adjust your attitude is the first step in self-leadership: you lead your frame of mind before anything else. Think about the attitudes you bring to the table as a leader, because they are vitally important to building a team that can get to greatness.

Leaders understand that what others call problems are simply Opportunities to GROW. So if you call it problem...then it will become problematic. If you see it as an opportunity to Grow...then a solution is easy to recognise.

ATTITUDE is a Product of BELIEF. You cannot have an attitude beyond your belief system. The

Lion is the King of the Jungle because of what he beliefs about himself and his superiority.

So the Power of your future is inside you. God has placed it inside you. Nobody can live beyond the limits of their beliefs. So you need to develop a word-based belief system.

Your life is what you think it should be. You need to think differently to change the outcome of your reality. Nothing can ever substitute for the right attitude.

So your Leadership Development is determined by:

1. **Your perception of who you are.** - You must change your perception of who you are.

2. **Why you think you exist.** - You must understand the reason you exist in God. You have got to discover your purpose.

3. **Your sense of significance.** - You must increase your sense of significance. Discover you are important to the world. You must believe this.

These three things allow you to Package your gifts in a language of VALUE. People buy into Value more readily than to anything else. Your Potential is nothing if your Mentality is weak. That is why an Elephant can act like a sheep in front of a Lion.

You can never truly carry out the Mandate of Leadership if you don't have the Mentality of Leadership. What you THINK can be more powerful than what you DO. Doing with the wrong thinking/attitude will produce failure and mediocrity. So commit to think correctly. Think in the Word of God.

LEADERSHIP CAPSULE #1

"Only those who DARE TO FAIL greatly can ever achieve greatly. Whatever you will become in life is always behind God. He is already ahead of you. So be bold, be strong and birth that Future from within you."

My Reflection:

As a leader, you must make bold decisions. And as a transformational leader, you must be prepared to move ahead even when not all information is available. Waiting for all the details could lead to paralyses in leadership.

You have to be able to decide on the way forward with eighty to ninety percent of the information. Waiting for the perfect condition or all the facts before making a decision could either lead to no decision being taken or decision taken too late to be effective. You have to trust your instinct as a leader. Remember those who don't make mistakes don't make anything.

To lead is to be daring. To inspire is to be grounded and certain - in yourself, in your vision and of the people who are walking with you.

The stakes are high and there are many times that leaders find themselves at major crossroads; at the tipping point of a thrilling change or bold step that is equally terrifying. So you need to be daring.

True leaders are those who can change the status quo and attempt the unexpected. Make that decision today and fine tune as you go along. Leaders are daring and bold. Make that move today and become the leader you were born to be.

Write Your Reflections

LEADERSHIP CAPSULE #2

"A Leader Must BELIEF IN HIMSELF as a Leader. A true Leader does not need external validation of his gift to know they exist; he/she Must have self-belief. This is the confidence that allows others to begin to see you as you see yourself."

My Reflection:

The world is full of doubt. More people are increasingly more doubtful in a rapidly confusing landscape in the Marketplace. The world is crying for leaders. People who will provide direction.

So a leader cannot look to the doubt-ridden world to validate himself. You have to belief in yourself. The certainty of your self-belief will compel others to agree with you. People will see you the way you see yourself. So you cannot be considered a leader or treated as such if you do not belief in yourself. You also cannot thrive in a position unless you see yourself in that position.

Confidence is the cornerstone of leadership. You can teach a leader to be an effective problem solver; more decisive; a better communicator; how to coach, mentor and hold team members accountable; and many other fundamentals of leadership. Yet, without that leader first believing in himself or herself, true leadership will exist only in title.

Belief in yourself also increases your creativity. If you accept yourself as a leader, you will be able to dig deeper into yourself to find solutions worthy of a leader. That brings creativity.

So stop doubting yourself. Stand strong. Accept your leadership calling and become a star in your world. Yes, you can!

Write Your Reflections

LEADERSHIP CAPSULE #3

"Good Leadership requires SELF-DEVELOPMENT. Just because someone made you the Boss doesn't also mean that they made you smarter than you were. A true Leader will continuously develop himself to justify and evidence the judgement that put him in office."

My Reflection:

Have you ever looked at your boss and wondered to yourself; *"Who promoted you?"* or *"How have you not been fired by now?"* If you have, take comfort in knowing you're not alone -- many of people have to deal with bosses that seem in over their heads on a daily basis.

There is a theory in management known as the PETER's PRINCIPLE. This was named after Dr Laurence J. Peter, who first stated this in his 1969 book.

Dr Peter stated that; *"In a hierarchy, every employee tends to rise to his level of incompetence,"* and that *"In time, every post tends to be occupied by an employee who is incompetent to carry out its duties."* So basically this is how it works: We do a job well, we're promoted. We do that job well, we're promoted again.

This happens in succession until we eventually rise to a position that we can no longer do well - - or our level of incompetence. There, we either stagnate, revert back to a lower position, or are fired.

As a leader you have to avoid this by constantly developing yourself. You cannot assume that the competences, skill and knowledge that sustained you at your previous level will do so at your new level. You must constantly add value to yourself. Develop yourself. Acquire new skills. Undergo new training. Read new books. Get a new mentor. Never sit still in the palace of knowledge. Avail yourself of every opportunity to become better at whatever you do. Simply because you were appointed or elected into a leadership position does not mean you can perform at that level. You have to raise your game as you raise your stage.

What have you done to improve yourself as a leader lately? Do you have a plan to develop yourself as a leader? Leadership skills are not automatic. They are learned and acquired. Invest in yourself as a leader. Leaders are learners.

Write Your Reflections

LEADERSHIP CAPSULE #4

"Your leadership capability should NOT BE BASED SOLELY ON YOUR TITLE. Your team members will develop respect for you based on how they see you operate, not solely on your position. People are interested in knowing how you solve problems."

My Reflection:

There is different basis on which people relate to leaders. Some is out of respect and admiration. Others relate purely out of fear of what the leaders can do by virtue of their position.

Leaders are supposed to inspire and influence people. True leaders will be accepted regardless of their title. In fact, people will duffer to people they consider leadership quality, regardless of their title. For you to be an effective leader, you cannot rely purely on your title. You must behave and motivate like a leader. Your title will not matter if you are a true leader of people.

Oftentimes, people confuse position, title and authority with leadership. The best leaders don't lead from position or authority. Leadership is not an actual position or title. Whether you're the president, a chief executive officer or a manager, your title will not make you a leader. Whilst position, title and authority provide you with the potential to lead, they do not make you a leader.

If you do not inspire people and have not earned their respect; they will only relate with you out of fear until you are no longer in that position. They you will lose all respect from the people.

True leaders like Nelson Mandela, remained a leader of people regardless of the title he had or not have. Mandela was equally influential and admired after his term as President of South Africa. Some even believe he became more admired after his term of office.

Bad leaders rely only on their title for obedience and compliance. They command respect only out of the fear people have of their power due to their current title or position. This kind of leadership do not endure.

Leadership is not about a title or a designation. It's about impact, influence and inspiration. Impact involves getting results, influence is about spreading the passion you have for your work in ways that inspire willing compliance. So leadership respect has to be earned. It will not be by simply being given a title.

So how do you lead at the moment? Do you rely only on your title or office to lead? If yes, you are not a true leader. Your office should not matter if you inspire and motivate people; they will follow you. Ask yourself; will people follow your advice or lead if you are not occupying your current position? Adjust and change as a leader.

Using title, authority and position is a poor way to influence others. It encourages people to rely on command and control as a means of getting things done. Leading from position has the following negative outcomes:[7]

- Leading from position undermines the development of relationships.
- Leading from position encourages negative political behaviours.
- Leading from position crushes the human spirit.
- Leading from position results in compliance.
- Leading from position frustrates creativity and innovation.
- Leading from position erodes trust.
- Leading from position produces mediocre results.

Leading from position and leveraging command and control results in lazy "leadership". Those who lead from position don't invest the time and energy required to establish a shared vision, to facilitate buy-in, to motivate and inspire others. Those who lead from position tend to hide behind

---

[7] http://goodadvice.com

company process and procedures, explaining why this or that can't be done.[8]

"All the effective leaders I have encountered – both those I worked with and those I merely watched – knew four simple things: a leader is someone who has followers; popularity is not leadership, results are; leaders are highly visible, they set examples; leadership is not rank, privilege, titles or money, it is responsibility." – Peter Drucker

---

[8] ibid

Write Your Reflections

LEADERSHIP CAPSULE #5

"Only Secure Leaders GIVE POWER TO OTHERS. A leader that does not delegate is insecure and will be unproductive. Wisdom of leadership will tell you that you cannot do everything. So learn to FOCUS ON WHAT IS MOST IMPORTANT and allow others to develop around you."

My Reflection:

The true measure of a leader is not in having followers; but in raising and developing other leaders. You cannot develop others if you do not delegate. Good leaders empower others, through responsibility. This means you have to accept others may not do it as well as you but you are prepared to accept their mistakes and occasional sub standard performance as price worth paying to develop them and raise their performance. A good leader knows he/she cannot do everything. So focus on what is important and allows others to learn and grown under you.

Delegation is a key and fundamental hallmark of good leadership. The ability to wisely and effectively delegate is a quality most crucial to a leader's success. Whether you're a manager at work, owner of your own business, effective delegation is one of the keys to achieving your goals.[9]

A man who insists on maintaining all control and authority is insecure and actually fails to even meet the definition of a good leader. A leader is an executive, a man who manages time, resources, and people. A leader does not do everything himself, rather he marshals all of these elements on the pathway to success.

Delegating frees you up to tackle the truly important aspects of your mission. Too many leaders, believing only they are able to do things just right, insist on being involved in every single

---

[9] http://www.artofmanliness.com/

detail of their missions. They believe that this ultra-hands-on approach is good for business because they're making sure everything gets done just right.

But a leader should be in charge of the overall direction of a team; he is the one looking ahead, steering the course, and making needed corrections to avoid getting off track. But buried in the small details, a man will lose the big picture and fail to see that the mission is falling apart until it is too late.

A good leader isn't a slave to detail; he uses his valuable time to tackle what's truly important. And this leads to greater success for him and his organization.[10]

So what kind of a leader are you? Do you delegate? Do you empower your followers? How good are you at delegating? You need to begin to inspire the direction of travel, but allows others to drive the delivery based on their skill and training.

---

[10] ibid

This will empower your team and motivate better performance.

"Mr. Garvin wanted Lloyd George back as Prime Minister. 'He's an old man,' said 72-year-old Mr. Garvin, 'but he's a genius.' And genius is like radium-it is radium always, no matter how little there is of it left...Perhaps Lloyd George can work only six hours a day, but six hours of Lloyd George is worth days of anyone else's month. In the last war Lloyd George knew had to delegate authority. He cared nothing for the political convictions of the men to whom he delegated it, only how they did their war job. That is what Chamberlain cannot do: delegate authority to able captains." **Life Magazine, 1940**

Write Your Reflections

LEADERSHIP CAPSULE #6

"Good Leaders must know HOW TO CONNECT WITH PEOPLE and their situations. Transformational Leaders Touch a Heart Before They Ask for a Hand. You must be genuinely interested in people and not what you want from them."

My Reflection:

Leaders are people-focused. They love people. They empathise. They feel for their people. Connecting with people on an individual level is crucial to leaders commanding loyalty and commitment.

You develop credibility with people when you connect with them and show them that you genuinely want to help them. The tougher the challenge for the leader, the greater the connection must be with his followers.

A key to connecting with others is recognizing that even in a group, you have to relate to people as individuals. It is often asked, "What is the secret to effectively speaking in front of large audiences of thousands of people?" The secret is simple. Do not try to talk to the thousands. Focus on talking to one person. That's the only way to connect with people.

It's the leader's job to initiate connection with people. Never underestimate the power of building relationships with people before asking them to follow you.

John Maxwell is known for his famous quote *"People don't care how much you know, until they know how much you care"* and that is a fact that should always remain at the back of our minds. When a leader has done the work to connect with his people, you can see it in the way the organization functions.

Among employees there is incredible loyalty and a strong work ethic. The vision of the leader becomes the aspiration of the people. The impact is incredible. There's an old saying: To lead yourself, use your head; to lead others, use your heart.

You can't move people to action unless you first move them with emotion. The heart comes before the head.

What opportunities do you provide for your team to communicate? How free are your followers to discuss and communicate with you? Do you value people on an individual level when you relate with them?

Learning the names of people who work for you (at least in your immediate circle) for instance, is an instant connector with them when you see them. It shows you see them as an individual rather than just a number amongst many. Learn to connect with people and grow in your leadership skill and competence.

Write Your Reflections

LEADERSHIP CAPSULE #7

"A leader is one who SEEKS RESPONSIBILITY, not Authority. Authority comes as we fulfil our responsibilities with a servant's heart and a humble attitude."

My Reflection:

Impact and influence are essential traits of good leadership. But these comes when you take responsibility for a situation and outcome. Authority dispenses power but there is no certainty of a desired outcome being achieved.

So a leader who simply exercises authority can end up just throwing his weight around without achieving any objective, talk less of motivating others to lead. Responsibility is essential to commend leadership. That is why in the medieval times, kings led their people to war.

They don't just sit back in the palace and send their soldiers out to war. They lead from the front. Such sense of responsibility built loyalty in the soldiers that were ready to fight to the death.

Jack Zenger in a Forbes magazine contribution titled, *"Taking Responsibility is the Highest Mark of Great Leaders"* stated that:
"Some might think that being responsible is the same thing as being accountable. But my later research suggests these are quite different mind-sets.

Being accountable means you are answerable and willing to accept the outcomes or results of a project or activity. But responsibility goes much further. It is the mind-set that says, "I am the person who must make this happen," whether it stems from your belief or because your job requires this of you, or there is some social force binding you to this obligation."

The only time it is okay, as a leader, to share responsibility is in success. To seek and take responsibility effectively you must strike balance in a couple of key areas.

You must find opportunities that stretch you but not break you. Also, you must maintain full responsibility in failure while knowing when to share it in success.

The problems you solve could define your leadership legacy. So what responsibilities have you taken on in your current position?

Do you accept responsibility for the outcome of your mission? Do not blame your followers. You are not yet a failure until you blame someone else. Take ownership and lead. Step up to take the hard tasks. Take ownership and make your impact felt.

Write Your Reflections

LEADERSHIP CAPSULE #8

"People BUY INTO THE LEADER, Then the Vision of the Leader. So a good vision can die because of bad leadership. A CREDIBLE LEADER is vital to selling a Vision as credible."

My Reflection:

A good and credible leader will easily sell an average vision to people, but a bad leader will not be able to sell an exceptional vision. People buy into you as a leader FIRST before they buy into your vision.

You cannot just rely on the strength of your vision to secure buy-in from others. You the visionary must be credible and appealing before your vision will stand a chance. Getting support for your ideas, vision, and strategy requires that people buy into you first. This often takes time.

To build credibility with people, develop relationships with them, earn their trust by displaying character, integrity, and honesty, hold yourself to high standards and set good examples.

When you add value to your relationships your credibility with other people increases and builds the foundation for people to buy into you and your ideas. Credibility is a characteristic of a person who is perceived by others to be a trusted advisor, believable, and confident by exhibiting a high level of expertise in a certain subject or about a certain vision or assignment.

No matter how well articulated; it is impossible for others to see and understand your vision fully after you explain it. They tend not to be able to see your vision for what it is initially. So the only certain, visible thing they can see and measure is you. Their perception of your credibility will be transferred into their credibility of your vision.

For instance; If you have a vision for a luxury brand and going about selling the idea to others; the way you present yourself is bound to be part of their consideration of your credibility.

How do you dress? What car do you drive? These are bound to affect their willingness to buy into your vision. So you dress for where you are going, not where you are coming from.

Credibility of a leader is a function of many things. How credible are you for your vision to be received positively as a leader? Do you match your words with appropriate actions? Are you a person of your word? Do you portray confidence and respectability? How do you speak as a leader?

All these will affect your ability to sell your vision. It will also determine the willingness of others to follow you.

How well do you represent your vision? Will you follow yourself if it was not you? Given that you understand best your vision; do you embody the thrust of the vision or objective you wish to accomplish? Make yourself the first and most significant signpost for your vision.

Write Your Reflections

LEADERSHIP CAPSULE #9

"Leaders must learn to PRIORITISE. Good Leaders Understand That ACTIVITY is not necessarily ACCOMPLISHMENT. They avoid Treadmill mentality, where you are busy and active; yet going nowhere and making no forward progress."

My Reflection:

Good leaders embrace the diversity of style of working by the members of the team; while still focusing on the objective agreed with each team member.

Leaders have to look beyond the exterior. A staff that comes in first in the morning and leaves last in the evening may be the least productive member of the team. But a staff that does less hours may be the most productive. Leaders must avoid a treadmill mentality both in themselves and others. Activity does not equal productivity.

Leaders must see beyond the headlines. Working hard may not be working smart. As a leader, you should understand that you cannot do everything. So you must prioritise what saliently needs to be done and work of those first. Have measurable matrix for yourself and assess your effectiveness that way, not just by activities alone.

So how good are you at seeing beyond the external activities and headlines? As a leader, do you focus more on attendance record of your team rather than their productivity?

Are you more concerned that your team arrive in the office on time always, or are you focusing on their output, productivity and work objective accomplishments? Bad leaders simply mark register. They manage by "seeing the team members" in the office only. Productivity should be the objective and not mere attendance record. Seek to understand the style of your team members.

People work in different ways. Good leaders show enough flexibility in management in such a way as to bring the best out of every team member.

Write Your Reflections

LEADERSHIP CAPSULES #10

"Trust Is the Foundation of Lasting Leadership. If you ABUSE PEOPLE'S TRUST; you may forfeit the right to lead them and the ability to Influence change in them."

My Reflection:

In the Marketplace; there is loyalty born out of admiration for and trust of the leadership. But there is also loyalty that is not only shallow but put on due to the power of the leadership over you.

The latter, tend to be called "eye service". That is putting on a performance or appearance of diligence when the leader is around and watching; but work is abandoned once the leader is not around or not watching.

Trust in leadership make people to be diligent and work effectively regardless of whether the leader is watching or not. Your team members do not all have to like you; but they must all admire your integrity and fairness. They must all be able to trust you.

Measured at a point in time; Trust is a function of your past dealings with people and not your future activities. Are you a person of your word? Do you act fairly? Do you show genuine interest in people or do you just use them?

Do you empathise with others? Do you take interest in events in the personal lives of your team and seek to support where necessary? Are you a good listener?

These are some of the factors that create trust in leadership. If your team do not trust you, it will be difficult to lead them to achieve anything. Trust in leadership improves the use of initiatives by the team. They are more confident to take risk in support of the vision or project if they trust you.

Write Your Reflections

LEADERSHIP CAPSULES #11

"There is not one situation in life that you cannot learn from -- if you're willing to have your attitude changed. You can LEARN FROM ANYTHING, if you are willing to change your attitude."

My Reflection:

Learning, either from your own mistakes or that of others is key to improving your leadership skills and expertise. Mistakes can become your friend if you are committed to improving your leadership skills.

You will keep learning ways not to do it. Making the same mistakes over and over again makes for bad leadership as your followers will start to lose confidence in you.

Your positive attitude as a leader can be all that your team are holding on to in despairing situations. Leaders are life long learners. You must seek the *"learning moment"* from every disappointments and setbacks. This is vital for your improvement as a leader.

Change and improvement should be a constant in the life of a leader. This will say to your team they cannot afford to remain stagnant as well.

Are you a learner or do you pretend you know it all? Are you willing to change if you getter better facts? Do you give room for your team to make mistakes and learn accordingly?

It is futile to seek perfection from your team when you the leader do not own up to your mistakes and learn from them.

Write Your Reflections

LEADERSHIP CAPSULES #12

"The power you face is THE POWER YOU PERCEIVE. That is to say, the oppressor's power is YOUR PERCEPTION OF HIS POWER; the oppressor's power is your thought. The source of their power is in your mind. That is, if you do not think that a man has power over you, he has none."

My Reflection:

This reflection relates to those that try to oppress you as a leader. The oppressors of leaders do not have to be people above them; it can also include team members that try to make your life difficult.

But a lot of the influence people have over you are primarily the influence you allow them to have. You have to develop selective deafness as a leader.

You have to know how to shut people out and not respond to their every move. Like bullies, oppressors and detractors thrive on your response being in line with their expectation. If your response surprises them, they lose the control they had over you. You must learn to ignore the bait of your detractors.

As a leader, you have to decline to give bad people power over you. You must focus on your assignment and refuse to be distracted. Everyone tries to influence the leader; those above you and those below you. You must identify your end goal and only work to advance your purpose.

You cannot afford to fight every battle and still move forward. Learn to ignore people that seek to get under your skin. Remain in control and demonstrate that they do not have power over you.

So as a leader, are you allowing the criticism or opinion of detractors bother you? Are you consumed by the view of others about you? Do not let the words of others affect you. Do not give others power over your peace and happiness. Do not outsource your confidence and contentment. That is what makes you a good leader.

Write Your Reflections

LEADERSHIP CAPSULES #13

"Some things are not necessarily wrong, THEY'RE JUST NOT NECESSARY. Some things are lawful ... but not necessary or character building. So you don't have to do everything. Selection is the name of the game. There are some jobs that should never be done. Some letters that should never be written & books that should never be read. You don't have time for everything. You must recognize what's important."

My Reflection:

Being able to know what are the important tasks and activities out of the myriads of demands on you is a crucial leadership skill. You cannot do everything. In addition to delegation of tasks, you must understand that there are tasks that need to be abandoned altogether. Either because they are peripheral to your main goal or they simply do not add any value to you mission.

Unnecessary tasks can easily become yokes round your neck as a leader. Know the wood from the trees. Do not mix them up.

How effective are you at ignoring unimportant tasks and demand on you as a leader? Are you able to understand the difference between essential tasks and fringe tasks?

You will burn out and fizzle out as a leader if you think every demand are equally important. They are not.

Develop a sense of balance and equilibrium. Know what is important, know what can wait. Prioritise and pace your performance. That will give you enough energy to be most effective in leadership.

Write Your Reflections

LEADERSHIP CAPSULES #14

"The Right decision can become the Wrong decision if it is made too late.....TIMELINESS IS PART OF THE JUDGEMENT involved in making the right decisions as a leader."

My Reflection:

If given unlimited time, and unlimited attempts, anyone will eventually make the right decision. Leadership is about timely decision making. As times and season change, business environment, political and economic condition changes. So a delayed decision can become the "right" thing done at the "wrong" time. Hence a wrong outcome is inevitable. Leaders have to trust their training and instinct in making decisions sometimes.

There will be times when the full picture is not clear and all the elements are not in place; yet you have to make a decision. Waiting for all the dots to line up may take time and you do not always have the time as a leader. So you get used to timely (not rushed) decision making as a leader.

How are you at making decisions? Do you take all the time while trying to make decisions? Are you the type of person that must know all the facts before making a decision or taking a risk? Can you make decision based on most of the facts or do you always want all the facts? The needs of your business or project may not allow for the time you seek to consider your choices. A good leader makes the best decision based on the best available facts at his/her disposal. That is all that is asked of you.

Highly admired leaders are decisive. They are ready to handle tough calls quickly and gracefully. Do you dither when it comes to making decisions? Are you decisive? Timeliness of decision can be the only determining factor in the successful outcome of that decision. A good decision made at the wrong time or too late will lead to bad outcomes.

Write Your Reflections

LEADERSHIP CAPSULES #15

"Just as you cannot steer or direct a stationary ship or car; God cannot direct you if you are stationary and without a plan. It is EASIER TO STEER A MOVING VEHICLE. So get up today and begin to act on your plans and see God step in to direct and steer you to Leadership victory."

My Reflection:

One of the things that differentiates a leader is that he acts while others just talk about it. A leader knows the value of starting work on a plan that is ninety percent than waiting for hundred percent detail before acting. Some blanks can be filled in while on the journey. It is easier to shape your destination while in motion than to remain motionless.

Procrastination is the thief of time as the popular saying goes. So stop procrastinating today. Embark on your leadership journey and watch how life will respond to steer you to the right destination as long as you are malleable and a willing to learn.

It is easier to steer an object that is moving that one that is static. As a leader there are many decisions that you may need to be making on a daily, weekly or monthly basis. You cannot afford to become undecided or just coast along. Purposeful motion is the building block for effective leadership.

Momentum is a good goal for a leader. Making little baby-steps progress is always better than stagnation. How good are you at moving things forward even when the whole picture is not yet clear? Get a sense of direction and move your mission forward. Changes are easier to make as you move than when inactive. You also gain better perspective as you see more widely as you make progress. This adds to the quality of your subsequent decisions.

Write Your Reflections

LEADERSHIP CAPSULES #16

"A Leader's Potential is determined by those closest to him. You cannot function as a Leader beyond the BIAS AND STRENGTH OF THOSE CLOSEST TO YOU. Be careful who you surround yourself with."

My Reflection:

Every leader cannot succeed alone. You need support and helpers and collaborators. Hence, the quality of those that surround you will be reflected in the quality of your decision.

Every person in your life exert influence over you one way or another otherwise they will not remain in your inner circle for too long. A good leader will surround himself with people that have wisdom and strength for the journey ahead.

Their perspectives will influence yours, so choose wisely who makes it into your inner circle.

As the going gets tough in leadership, you come to rely more on the advice and suggestions of those close to you. If they were badly chosen in the first place; you will end up with poor quality counsel and end in failure.

A leader cannot see every thing or know every angle. That is why he needs to be surrounded by those that can see what he does not see and know what he may not know. This confluence of good and knowledgeable advice broadens the pool the leader can fish from for meaningful solution.

Misinterpretation is a common problem with people in general but it is even a bigger problem for leaders. How you see things is mostly a reflection of your internal issues and perceptions rather than the actual truth of the situation.

This can lead to wrong perspective and wrong leadership behaviour. This is why you must surround yourself with good advice-givers in your inner circle. They can help create a balance for you and help navigate away from avoidable cataracts.

As a leader, you'll be constantly influencing people, but as a person, you yourself will be constantly influenced by those in your surroundings. So who do you surround yourself with currently? Do they compliment you? Are you aware of the biases of your inner circle? Choose wisely who you give your ears to as a leader.

Write Your Reflections

LEADERSHIP CAPSULES #17

"The Paradox of Leadership requires you to speak the truth and correct others, even though you are work in progress yourself. You will never be able to lead; if you feel you must be PERFECT FIRST BEFORE YOU CAN DIRECT OTHERS. The truth does not change simply because it is declared by an imperfect vessel."

My Reflection:

A common misconception in budding leaders is that they must achieve perfection or proficiency on an issue before they can direct others on that same issue.

The thinking is that it will be hypocritical to demand of others what you have not yet achieved yourself. This is far from reality. If all leaders wait until they have perfected an act before demanding same from others; nothing will ever be achieved. All leaders are work in progress.

You are always getting better at something. You are always fine-tuning yourself in one thing or another. Your imperfection in an area should not stop you saying or doing what is right by others.

For instance, a leader that is battling with alcohol and getting help to stop drinking, can still tell others drinking is bad for them. It is not hypocrisy. I call it the paradox of leadership. The truth remains the truth regardless of who is saying it.

Leaders must learn to say the truth and pursue best practice even if they are not fully compliant yet themselves. A leader is not perfect so as such must have a personal battle he is fighting at any point in time. That battle does not disqualify him from speaking on the same matter and correcting others and warning them not to make the same mistake. So you have a duty to say the truth and correctly train others, regardless of your personal battle or challenges.

Write Your Reflections

LEADERSHIP CAPSULES #18

"A good leader must be self aware enough to KNOW THE ROLES OF THE DIFFERENT PEOPLE in his life. Not all the people in your camp are for you, but you must know who is who. Get it wrong and you can make a shipwreck of your leadership".

My Reflection:

Great leadership is not just about people; it is also about self-discovery. A great leader knows that people are not attracted to him, but to his gift. Don't be fooled. People are not always so much in love with you. It is about your gift not you. The same people who claim to adore you today can call for your head tomorrow.

There are usually three kinds of people that will confront you as a leader.

CONFIDANTS: These are people who are for you period. They stay with you regardless of what you do. They will visit you in prison if you end up there. They are mentors and protégés. If you find a handful of these people in your lifetime, then you are truly fortunate. They are very few in number.

CONSTITUENTS: They are not for you; but they are for what you are for. They identify with your Mission and Goals. They will stay until that mission is accomplished or more likely until they find someone else who can better articulate that Mission; then they shift camp. They are not into you as a person per se; they are into what you are doing or pursuing. They share your goals not your destiny. Most will leave you at one point or another; and sometimes at the most inconvenient time. But do not be worried as they were never into you to start with.

COMRADES: These types of friends are not for you and neither are they for what you are for. But they are against what you are against. You share a common enemy. They will stay with you only until victory is won or until they give up the fight.

Everybody you know will fall into these three categories. And don't be fooled to think your family members are your natural confidants. You will be sadly disappointed. Family members can be in all three categories, so you will need to discern who is who. Some of the most painful wounds in life has been inflicted by family members.

So how do you identify your Confidants? A few tips (by no means all the tips):

> They will be genuinely happy for you when you are happy.
> They will share your disappointments and life's lows.
> They are not prone to telling you only what you want to hear; they tell you what they believe you need to hear. So they are not praise-singers or yes-men.
> Confidants act as critical friends.
> They will safeguard your confidentiality when you entrust them with your secrets.
> They stay with you and declare it long after many have left you.

115

➤ They will not be offended by your weaknesses; but will be determined to help you overcome it.

➤ Distance makes no difference to the depth and quality of this relationship.

➤ A confidant will fight your corner even before hearing your side of the story.

➤ A confidant believes in you even when you don't believe in yourself.

➤ A True confidant will always remind you of the need for God in your life.

I hope your paths will cross that of your true confidants as a leader and you will learn to understand the values of each of these categories of friends.

You cannot fulfil your vision with confidants alone. And you cannot do so without them either. So you need the skill and focus of comrades when there is a common enemy to overcome and you need the service and enthusiasm of constituents to drive visions into fulfilment. Just understand who is who and understand many will leave at their own time and not yours.

Write Your Reflections

LEADERSHIP CAPSULES #19

"The right Mentality is what wakes up the Leadership Spirit within you. Without DEVELOPING THE RIGHT ATTITUDE; you will never activate the spirit within you."

My Reflection:

As stated in my introduction to this book, having the right attitude in life is important, but more so having the right attitude in leadership. Attitude is in the realm of choice, meaning that you can control it at any point in time, no matter the circumstances you are facing.

In fact, learning to adjust your attitude is the first step in self-leadership: you lead your frame of mind before anything else. Think about the attitudes you bring to the table as a leader, because they are vitally important to building a team that can get to greatness.

Having the right attitude towards life is imperative if we want to see leadership success. The attitude of the leader has a huge impact on the culture, environment, and mood of the department or organisation. The leader's attitude tends to spread and affect others dramatically.

It does not matter how educated you are, how qualified you are; it's your mind that keeps you small. Just as it does not matter how unqualified you feel; it's your Mind that makes you a Leader. The key is attitude. It is attitude that differentiates Leaders from Followers. Your attitude conditions your response and posture. Your attitude is a product of what you see. Change your view.

Your attitude will be contagious. Those around you are likely to follow your lead. When a leader is upbeat in the face of discouraging circumstances, others admire that quality and want to be like him. So you need to belief in yourself as a leader. Develop the right mentality that allows you to be confident as a leader.

A leader must not allow himself to become paralysed by a crisis. Neither must a leader allow his team to notice that they are confounded by a situation. Certainly a leader will be concerned by circumstances, and maybe even share that concern among his team, but the leader won't stop there. The leader will develop a plan and press on. That is the right attitude.

Write Your Reflections

LEADERSHIP CAPSULES #20

"The Greatest enemy of Progress is your last Success......KEEP LOOKING FORWARD. Leaders should inspire performance for continuous success."

My Reflection:

Leaders with strong reputations are scouted to turn around struggling teams in many organisations. Past success is frequently used as a measuring stick for someone's future potential.

However, there is a danger that comes with past success, particularly in complex environments. In a constantly changing world that requires experimentation and change, past success can make you more vulnerable to failure.

This is because it makes you more likely to stick with a way of operating that no longer applies. This can mean disaster on an organisational level. Success can be a dangerous thing. It can lull you into a dangerous, and very wrong, pattern of thinking that whatever you've done thus far will continue. Throughout history, those who thought that things would always continue as they are, have inevitably been proven wrong.

If care is not taken, past success can breed arrogance and complacency. So as a leader you must keep looking forward. Keep looking ahead to new challenges and how you can improve yourself, your team and your project or tasks.

A perfect definition from Garry Kasparov's 'Winter is Coming':

"Each victory pulls the victor down slightly and makes it harder to put in maximum effort to improve further. Meanwhile, the loser knows that he made a mistake, that something went wrong, and he will work hard to improve for next time. The happy winner often assumes he won simply because he is great. Typically, however, the winner is just the player who made the next-to-last mistake. It takes tremendous discipline to overcome this tendency and to learn lessons from a victory."

Write Your Reflections

LEADERSHIP CAPSULES #21

"You cannot be a leader until you hate something or angry at something. This is what DRIVES YOUR PASSION for action."

My Reflection:

You decide to become a leader when you can't take it anymore and you apply yourself to a solution through sacrifice. Passion is essential in leadership. People need to see you stand for something. That you are driven by certain values and passion for specific change.

Passion is a key element for a leader. The people who are successful and achieve great things have passion. It is important to find the areas you are passionate about then stay focused on them. I have discovered finding your purpose and strengths helps when it comes to having passion. Passion can influence your leadership effectiveness in several ways:[11]

1. **Passion produces energy** - A leader who has passion is driven forward from the energy it produces. When it comes to leading yourself and others passion and energy are essential. Donald Trump said, *"Without passion you don't have energy, without energy you have nothing."* Leaders who have passion also bring energy into what they do.

2. **Passion drives vision** - If a leader wants to see their vision and goals being accomplished, then the leader's passion is the fuel that drives the production and results of the vision. The vision of the organisation or team should be frequently and passionately communicated to others.

3. **Passion ignites others** – If you have ever been around a passionate leader, you will notice that their energy and passions robs off on you. This causes you to feel more energised and motivated.

---

[11] http://danblackonleadership.info/archives/1273

A leader's passions can ignite other people's passions and bring energy into their life.

4. **Passion raises influence-** John Wesley said, *"When you set yourself on fire, people love to come and see you burn."* This is what happens when a leader has passion. The leader starts gaining more influence with others and people want to be a part of what's going on. If you want to raise your influence, then you need to be a passionate leader.

5. **Passion provides potential-** A leader's passion brings new opportunity and opens the door to success. This is because when you're passionate about what you're doing it moves you closer to your potential. Moving you closer to your potential causes you to be moving into the next level within your career and personal journey.

It's the passionate people that take the biggest risks, step up to the plate, and help make the biggest leaps forward within teams, companies, and organisations. Passion for the projects, for the company and for the people involved are key to successful leadership.

So the question for you today is, have you found your passions and how do they impact your leadership and life?

Write Your Reflections

LEADERSHIP CAPSULES #22

*"A good leader must recognise his prejudice. We all have some. **RECOGNITION OF YOUR BIASES is** essential to mitigate it in decision making. A leader must know when his own prejudice is colouring his judgement so as to act. Being self aware is indispensable to becoming a great leader".*

My Reflection:

In leadership capsule number 16, we looked at how the biases of those surrounding a leader can affect the leader. But this capsule addresses the biases of the leader himself. Everybody have biases and prejudices. These are products of our upbringing and societal exposures.

But as a leader you need to be able to control your biases in ways that you do not act based on them. The first step is to know you have the biases and preconceptions as an individual. Once you acknowledge that; you can begin to take steps to ensure your decisions as a leader is not affected by them. This requires a great deal of self awareness.

Knowledge is power. The more information you have that is objective and fact based; the more you can overrule your prejudice in making decisions. For example, if you were brought up to believe that women cannot perform certain tasks and should therefore not be appointed to certain roles. That is your prejudice.

But the more information you acquire to debunk that prejudice; the easier it will be to overrule your preconceived disposition in this area as you will now act based on a superior knowledge you have assimilated and not on the residual information you got growing up.

Also knowing your biases allows you to surround yourself with people who will help mitigate your weaknesses in those areas. Do you know your biases? You need to know yourself fully as a leader.

Write Your Reflections

LEADERSHIP CAPSULES #23

"Good leaders DON'T RAISE FOLLOWERS but other leaders. You must influence others positively and shape them based on your enduring values. Your true claim to immortality is the quality of life you live, how many lives you touch and PUTTING SUCCESSION PLAN in place."

My Reflection:

Great leaders are those whose vision and ventures outlast them. They have succeeded in pouring themselves into other leaders they reproduced and those in turn runs with the vision as if it was their own idea.

Succession planning is essential in leadership. It is a sign of bad leadership if the show has to stop when you are not around. There are some organisations that nothing can progress until the boss comes back from holiday as nobody can make decisions in his absence. This is unacceptable.

Your primary goal as a leader is to raise other leaders and not just to create followers. Succession planning begins when you focus on raising people who can do what you do and even do it better.

So you have to invest in others, train them, equip them and give them opportunities to make decisions on their own; to be able to develop successors in any area of life where you lead.

Succession planning is a deliberate and systematic effort by an organization to ensure leadership continuity in key positions, retain and develop intellectual and knowledge capital for the future, and encourage individual advancement.

Succession planning also helps prevent dictatorships. Recognising that you will not always be there should inspire you to raise others who will carry the mission forward long after you are gone. This is the hallmark of great leadership in the marketplace. Managing your talent pipeline is essential for business continuity in the marketplace.

From an organisational viewpoint, there are four basic stages to developing succession plan.

Phase 1: *Identify Key/Critical Business or Project Positions*

Phase 2: *Conduct Position Analysis*

Phase 3: *Develop Succession Plan*

Phase 4: *Monitor, Evaluate, Review*

Developing the potentials of your team will not only bring role satisfaction to them but it will also make them more committed to the organisation and deliver their best performance.

Do you have a succession plan for your organisation or project? Can the show go ahead in your absence or everything depends on your presence in the office? Plan well and develop other leaders.

Write Your Reflections

LEADERSHIP CAPSULES #24

"Creativity is the hallmark of a good leader. Being able to find CREATIVE AND INNOVATIVE SOLUTIONS to complex problems makes you excel as a leader. So shine as a leader through creativity."

My Reflection:

Leaders are creative and innovative. Creativity is not a gift just given to certain 'arty' types of people. Neither is it a personality type, a particular kind of event or a notable work of art.

Creativity is our God given nature; the creator of the universe has downloaded himself into people. Creativity is within our special DNA code; we are all creative by divine nature. We may not all be expressing it, but we already have it and must harness it to be a good leader"

Innovative leadership is always creative. Innovation is the application of a new idea that results in a valuable improvement. This definition protects us from people thinking that innovation is just lots of useless ideas. If it can't be used to improve what we do, it's not truly innovative.

Innovation is more needed in leadership now than ever before. Leaders need innovation. They need it for themselves as they learn to operate in challenging, unpredictable circumstances. They also need to create a climate for innovation within organisations. Innovative systems, tools, and thinking are essential for organisational health and future viability in the marketplace.

Given the various and rapid changes in our world, leaders throughout organisations know they need to change the way they work. As they seek to drive results at a tactical level, leaders are looking for new rules of the road to give them a competitive edge and fuel new industries, markets, products, and services.

To make effective sense of unfamiliar situations and complex challenges, we must have a grasp of the whole of the situation, including its variables, unknowns, and mysterious forces. This requires skills beyond everyday analysis. It requires innovation leadership. Are you innovative?

To grasp this concept of innovation in leadership; there are two basic proposition you need to understand. First is *an innovative approach to leadership*. This means to bring new thinking and different actions to how you lead, manage, and go about your work.

The second is; *leadership for innovation*. This means leaders must learn how to create an organisational climate where others apply innovative thinking to solve problems and develop new products and services. It is about growing a culture of innovation.

This two-tiered approach or proposition generates the kind of innovation that can deal with any challenges you or your organisation may face in the modern marketplace landscape. *Are you an innovative leader? What can you do to become one?*

Write Your Reflections

LEADERSHIP CAPSULES #25

"Love is the foundation of any true Leadership effort. You cannot lead successfully people you do not love. GROW IN LOVE and you stand a good chance of growing in leadership grace."

My Reflection:

Love, sympathy and empathy are essential traits of a good leader. Leading people requires you to invest in others. This will be easier to do by a leader who loves the people he is leading.

Of course I am talking about normal human platonic and neighbourly love. A lover of humanity will always go the extra mile to get the best out of others. Your capacity to lead increase with your capacity to be compassionate and grow in love.

153

You will work with people who will have their various individual human challenges. So your ability to show understanding and compassion can transform a reluctant team member to a star worker who will give his best to the organisation or project you lead.

Whatever you actually do in the marketplace; in the end it all boils down to human relationships. How good are you at relating with others? Do you respect the people you work with?

Leaders who are full of love for their team will always get the best out of them. Are you such a leader?

Write Your Reflections

LEADERSHIP CAPSULES #26

"Leadership attitude can be a product of personal beliefs. Your belief system can influence your choices. It it hard to live beyond the limits imposed by your beliefs. So you need to DEVELOP A FITTING BELIEF SYSTEM for the success of your mission and keep your personal beliefs personal."

My Reflection:

We already stated how a leader must be self aware. Part of this process is knowing what your belief systems are. This is not just religious.

Your value system, cultural beliefs and of course religious beliefs affect your choices as a leader. So how do you operate as a leader but still be true to your beliefs. We are all predisposed to act in certain ways based on our beliefs. So a leader need to assess the suitability of his paradigms for the environment he functions. On one hand, beliefs are personal to each person. But it exerts influence on decisions and choices people make.

Firstly, a good leader should be sensitive to the beliefs of the people in his team and work with them in ways that get the best out of them. This will involve some flexibility on the part of the leader. For example, you as a leader may need to make accommodation for the dietary requirements of your team based on their beliefs at a business lunch.

Secondly, you must focus on the mission as the unifying factor for all your team. Don't use use your position to force your beliefs (of whatever kind) on your team. If they are inspired by your beliefs, soon enough they will voluntarily buy into it.

I know a very successful businessman who built and led a firm and made millions from being the biggest pork meat importer into a particular country. The thing is, this businessman is a devout Muslim. Islam forbids eating of pork but he was a great leader in the marketplace by not imposing his personal belief on the business. He led the team to belief in the success of the venture and they succeeded. Good leaders are mission focused.

Your dominant belief should be in the success of your mission, business or project. Give them a belief that success is achievable. You also need to be certain there are no limiting pull on your team from your personal beliefs. You must not make your belief an obstacle to your leadership success in the marketplace.

Write Your Reflections

LEADERSHIP CAPSULES #27

"Focus on main Goals. A Leader does not get himself BUGGED DOWN WITH PETTY SQUABBLING and minor imperfections of his team. He focuses on Outcomes and Substantive matters. People will still be true to themselves while you lead them, so expect diverse temperaments, but focus them on securing the outcome."

My Reflection:

One of the key causes of leadership failure is allowing distractions to creep in. Before long, you will be focusing on minor issues while neglecting your main tasks. Leaders must learn to overlook distractions and not allow side issues take away their focus.

You must also avoid the tyranny of the urgent. That is; focusing on what seems urgent while not doing what is important.

What is most important may not be urgent. And what is urgent may not be important at all. So do not allow yourself to be terrified by what seems urgent at the expense of important deliverables. Always focus on what is important first.

Be outcome-focused. Petty fights and disagreements should be avoided. There are so many little side developments that can derail perfectly laid plans.

Great leaders are those that can secure outcomes from people that are not like them. Managing people of different temperaments and paradigms can be a challenge for leaders.

Star Leaders know how to navigate through the mess of people's lives to bring out what is needed to deliver corporate objective. There is no bad team; only bad leader.

Sometimes in a team, the most gifted person is also the most flawed individual. A leader should know how to get the best out of such people while not allowing their flawed personality to be a distraction.

Are you able to overlook flaws in team members while still focusing their energy of agreed outcomes? To be a great leader; you have to be able to manage people of diverse temperaments.

Write Your Reflections

LEADERSHIP CAPSULES #28

"Good leaders view their team members with professional eyes rather than emotional. You will have team members who perform brilliantly but rubbish at human relations. Leaders must know how to harvest potential/result from people they may not like personally. Don't allow your EMOTION TO CLOUD YOUR JUDGEMENT."

My Reflection:

It is true that we are all emotional being, but good leaders will have to act in a cold and calculating way most of the time. You cannot afford to act purely based on emotion as a leader.

Emotion has the capacity to blind from objective facts. So a good leader must not be led by your emotion is making team decisions. Because emotion can be transient and fluctuating, it is not a good basis to make long term decision about business activities.

You may have to put your dislike of someone aside to approach him if he is the best brain in the team on a particular subject. Business decision must be rational and cool headed. You have to be professional. Workplace is not a social club. So your views have to remain professional in nature.

Write Your Reflections

LEADERSHIP CAPSULES #29

"To be most effective, you need to know what's going on without people spelling it out for you expressly. COLLECT UNSPOKEN DATA from body language and looks, given across meeting rooms to help you intuit the underlying messages."

My Reflection:

In the marketplace, every move you make tells a secret. A good leader cannot afford to wait to be expressly informed of developments. It may already be too late to save your project at that point.

You need to be able to gain information from unspoken words. You need to know the moods of your team. Know the state of your operation. This allows you to pick up changes in moods and step in early to help, support or provide any other intervention needed. Research has shown that less than ten percent of communication is verbal. Majority are non-verbal communications. Facial expressions, tone of voice, gesticulations, looks and so on, all communicate better than simply words. So a leader needs to be able to read the body language of his team and know when something is wrong at the earliest opportunity.

Body language can include any non-reflexive or reflexive movement of a part, or all of the body, used by a person to communicate an emotional message to the outside world. A good leader need to be intuitive about changes in the equilibrium of his team.

There will be many team members that may be reluctant to discuss some developments bothering them; but will appreciate your intuitive intervention and support as a leader. Are you intuitive? Are you good at picking up subtle signals? Read up, train up, so whatever you can to become better at reading people. This will be valuable not only in team management but also in negotiation with rivals and your supply chain.

Write Your Reflections

LEADERSHIP CAPSULES #30

"A good leader must BE DELIVERED FROM HIS PEOPLE before he can deliver his people. Leaders must be ready to make unpopular decisions. Many times you must be willing to convey the truth to people, no-matter who will get upset. This may lead to some temporary challenges, but a leader will become ineffective if paralysed by the opinion of the people he leads."

My Reflection:

Leading is not about popularity context, it is about inspiring people to appreciate what they may not value so that they will end up valuing what they appreciated.

A leader must be prepared to make decisions based on the overall interest of the business or project, even if that means overruling members of his team. What is popular may not be good. But in the end, what is good will end up being popular.

Tough love is a trait good leaders have. Leaders usually know more of the unifying assignment more than others; so you may have to make decisions that is leading the team. Some in the team may not agree with you because they do not see what you see. It is your job as leader to give directions and your choice may not be the most popular. Yet you still need your team to implement your directive, even though they may not be enthusiastic to start with.

You do not have to be popular, but be a good leader and generate good outcomes. Popularity will end up coming with the hindsight your successful results will create.

Are you afraid of your team? Are you too concerned about how others will feel? Be a leader. Be delivered from the opinions of your team. Make decisions that will change lives and situations for the better.

Write Your Reflections

OTHER RELEVANT BOOKS BY DR CHARLES OMOLE

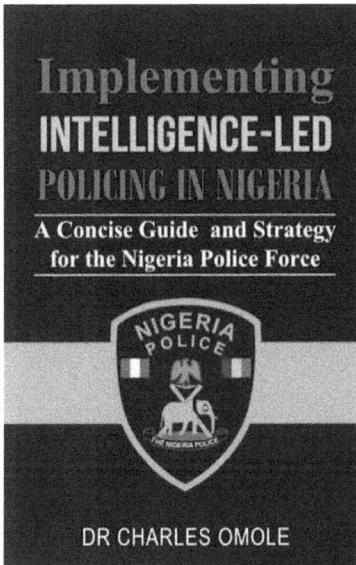

Implementing
INTELLIGENCE-LED
POLICING IN NIGERIA

**A Concise Guide and Strategy
for the Nigeria Police Force**

DR CHARLES OMOLE

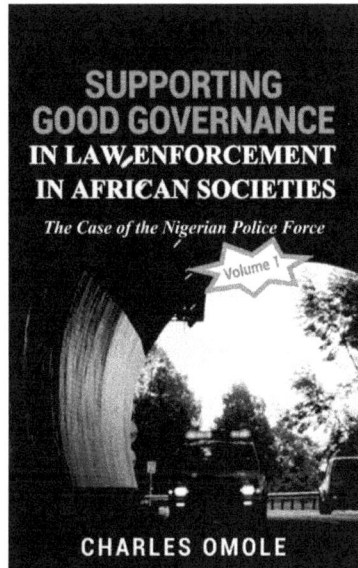

**SUPPORTING
GOOD GOVERNANCE
IN LAW ENFORCEMENT
IN AFRICAN SOCIETIES**

The Case of the Nigerian Police Force

Volume 1

CHARLES OMOLE

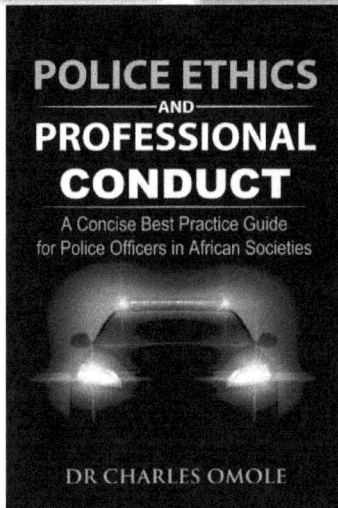

**POLICE ETHICS
—AND—
PROFESSIONAL
CONDUCT**

A Concise Best Practice Guide
for Police Officers in African Societies

DR CHARLES OMOLE

You can reach Dr Omole at:

Charlesomole@Gmail.com

www.ingramcontent.com/pod-product-compliance
Lightning Source LLC
Chambersburg PA
CBHW060026210326
41520CB00009B/1016